HEALING IS YOURS

WORKBOOK & JOURNAL

Freely Receive Healing Based On Jesus
Finished Work.
Includes Journal Prompts To Go Deep

CHRISTINA PERERA

THIS BOOK BELONGS TO:

_____

TABLE OF CONTENTS

Each section includes biblical teaching and journaling prompts to help you dive deep into God's Word, renew your mind, and receive healing by faith in Jesus' finished work.

CHRISTINA PERERA MINISTRIES

Radically Healed.

I would have lost heart, unless I had believed
That I would see the goodness of the Lord
In the land of the living.
Wait on the Lord;
Be of good courage,
And He shall strengthen your heart;
Wait, I say, on the Lord!

Psalm 27:13-14 NKJV

MY HEALING TESIMONY

It was a beautiful March spring day. My husband and I walked through the fields of a nearby park, our little chihuahua, Bubba, leading the way. Little did I know it was one of the last days of normalcy I would experience for the next seven years.

The next morning, I woke up suddenly sick, unable to move even an inch of my body without debilitating exhaustion and pain. I lay in bed, having no idea what was happening within my body. Over the next few years, I would earn an amateur degree in medicine and encounter the resurrected Jesus. Most of all, I would discover the power of a God who draws so near even in our darkest moments.

The next few months were spent in a swirl of confusion, fear, and pain. I was newly married and had my whole life ahead of me, and suddenly, I was a prisoner in my own body.

CHRISTINA PERERA MINISTRIES

ENCOUNTERING THE LIVING GOD

I couldn't function, move, think, or even form a sentence correctly. My body was giving up, and I was trapped inside, full of hopes, dreams, and what I thought was a full life.

Pain seized my joints and muscles, confusion, my thoughts, and fear gripped my heart. Although I was a believer, I could hardly pray. I just wept before the Lord for answers.

I began to seek answers for my new reality. My first step was to my primary care physician, who, a few blood tests later, discovered that my body was duplicating blood cells incorrectly with damaged DNA.

Also, I suddenly developed three different auto-immune conditions overnight. My immune system was going awry, but why?

Many years passed, and many doctor appointments.

I had many opportunistic infections, including Lyme, and my immune system, instead of attacking viruses and bacteria, was attacking me.

But in the midst of all of these circumstances, the God of all hope made His presence so known to me.

I had a friend who told me about the baptism of the Holy Spirit. Although I had grown up in the church, I had never heard of this. My heart immediately cried out, "God, if this is you, I want this!"

We prayed for the baptism of the Holy Spirit outside of an ice cream shop. She quickly prayed laying her hands on me and said, "Now speak in tongues!" I said the first thing that came out of my mouth, and she beamed delightedly, "Good, you got it!"

The next morning, I awoke to the presence of God hovering in my bedroom, and I had an insatiable desire for the Word of God.

JESUS HAS THE LAST WORD

I remember weeping and weeping at God's goodness for tangibly being with me. I had grown up in a Baptist Church, so I had never encountered God's presence in such a tangible way.

I was filled with awe, wonder, and gratitude at a God that draws so near in times of need.

In that first moment, God's presence changed the game, and I began a journey of being radically transformed inside and out, renewing my entire being.

Jesus turned dark days into the most glorious ones simply by His presence. He delighted my heart daily as He taught me the gospel of the grace of Jesus Christ.

He spoke words of truth to my new identity in Christ. He healed my heart of past trauma, and introduced me to the kingdom of God.

He taught me the new covenant of grace and all that he had accomplished through the finished work of Christ! Through this transformative journey, He taught me how to receive by faith all I needed through Him.

I received healing to my immune system through a powerful encounter and was filled with the power of God to such extent there are no traces of blood cancer, autoimmune disease, or any other opportunistic infections. Praise Jesus!

Jesus is the great I AM, which means whatever you need, He will be for you. If you need a healer, He is your healer. If you need a deliverer, He is your deliverer. These next chapters contain the foundational truths that helped renew my mind about what Jesus has accomplished for us in the area of healing. As you read and journal through the pages, I pray that the God of all hope will meet you here!

Purpose of Sacrifice.

For the law, having a shadow of the good things to come, and not the very image of the things, can never with these same sacrifices, which they offer continually year by year, make those who approach perfect. For then would they not have ceased to be offered? For the worshipers, once purified, would have had no more consciousness of sins. But in those sacrifices there is a reminder of sins every year. For it is not possible that the blood of bulls and goats could take away sins.

Hebrews 10:1-4 NKJV

WE HAVE FALLEN SHORT

From the beginning, man walked with God upon the earth, enjoying the sweetness of fellowship between a created being and its creator. When the fall of man happened in Genesis, sin entered the world. For the first time, man became separated from God because of his sinful nature.

The Law of Moses was given on Mount Sinai to Moses, a mediator between God and the children of Israel, to communicate God's perfect standard of love. The Law of Moses consists of the Ten Commandments, and 613 additional laws were never designed to be used as justification for our righteousness.

The Bible clarifies that no man can stand before God and justify himself. No matter what good you have done, there are still places you have fallen short. *For all have sinned and fall short of the glory of God.* (Romans 3:23 NKJV)

THE PURPOSE OF THE LAW

So what was the purpose of the Law then? Let's see what the Bible says.

According to the apostle Paul, as written in the book of Galatians, the **Law was given so that the trespasses would increase because of the sin nature inherited through every human since Adam.**

Let's look at what Galatians 3:19-25 NKJV

What purpose then does the law serve? It was added because of transgressions, till the Seed should come to whom the promise was made; and it was appointed through angels by the hand of a mediator. Now a mediator does not mediate for one only, but God is one.
Is the law then against the promises of God? Certainly not! For if there had been a law given which could have given life, truly righteousness would have been by the law.

But the Scripture has confined all under sin, that the promise by faith in Jesus Christ might be given to those who believe. But before faith came, we were kept under guard by the Law, kept for the faith which would afterward be revealed. Therefore the Law was our tutor to bring us to Christ, that we might be justified by faith. But after faith has come, we are no longer under a tutor.

Thanks to Jesus, faith has now come, and we are justified from everything the Law could not justify us. To be justified means to be declared righteous, holy, and sanctified before God. What the Law could not do, Jesus Christ did in the sacrifice of the cross and resurrection.

Because all who trust Jesus have been declared righteous, Jesus rose from the dead, purging our sins once and for all.

Sacrifice & Offering Don't Please God.

Despite our human weakness and shameful failure to keep God's holy standard of love, God intervened on our behalf. The Father's love for the world is more significant than our sin and failures. He loves us so much that He sent His only Son Jesus to become the sacrifice for our sins and lawless deeds. Before we could ever choose Him, He chose us.

LETS GO DEEP!

How does it make you feel knowing your heavenly Father sent His only Son despite your failure to keep His glorious standards?

_____

_____

_____

_____

_____

_____

WHERE HAVE YOU FALLEN SHORT OF GOD'S STANDARDS?

Pick a moment in your life or action where you know you have fallen short of God's glorious standard of love.

_____

_____

_____

_____

_____

_____

_____

_____

_____

_____

Invite Jesus into that moment and allow Him to speak to your heart. Record what He is saying here.

_____

_____

_____

_____

_____

_____

How did Jesus change that experience for you?

JESUS The Perfect Lamb.

*The next day John saw Jesus coming toward Him, and said,
"Behold! The Lamb of God
who takes away the sin of the world!"*

John 1:29 NKJV

JESUS IS GOD'S LAMB

Under the Old Testament Law, God instituted an annual system of ceremonies, feasts, and sacrifices that would cover the sins for one year. Ultimatly, these sacrifices were to point the children of Israel to the coming Messiah, Jesus who would become the ultimate sacrifice for sin.

God did not desire animal sacrifices but the ultimate sacrifice that would forever blot out the sins of the worshipers. Let's explore what the Bible declares of Jesus from the book of Hebrews.

Therefore, when He came into the world, He said:

"Sacrifice and offering You did not desire, But a body You have prepared for Me. In burnt offerings and sacrifices for sin You had no pleasure. Then I said, 'Behold, I have come— In the volume of the book it is written of Me— To do Your will, O God.' " Hebrews 10:5-7 NKJV

ONE SACRIFICE ONCE FOR ALL

Let's continue reading in the book of Hebrews how God found fault with a system of annual sacrifice because it could not remove the consciousness of sin completely.

Previously saying, "Sacrifice and offering, burnt offerings, and offerings for sin You did not desire, nor had pleasure in them" (which are offered according to the law), then He said, "Behold, I have come to do Your will, O God."

He takes away the first that He may establish the second. By that will we have been sanctified through the offering of the body of Jesus Christ once for all. Hebrews 10:8-10 NKJV

God found fault with a system of annual sacrifices because they reminded us of our sins each year. He desires our consciences to be completely purged of any reminder of sin.

God the Father sent Jesus to be the perfect sacrifice; only the sinless blood of the Lamb of God could take away the sin from our conscience. Let's continue from the book of Hebrews.

And every priest stands ministering daily and offering repeatedly the same sacrifices, which can never take away sins. But this Man, after He had offered one sacrifice for sins forever, sat down at the right hand of God, from that time waiting till His enemies are made His footstool. For by one offering He has perfected forever those who are being sanctified. Hebrews 10:11-14 NKJV

Jesus was resurrected without your sin, having purged them from your life once for all. Therefore, you can be confident that your heavenly Father is satisfied with Jesus' work.

As a result, you can enjoy lasting peace with God and assurance that He will be gracious to you in time of need.

It Is Finished!

As a result of Jesus' perfect obedience to the will of the Father on the cross, we can rest assured that our sins and lawless deeds will be remembered no more!

Therefore, when He came into the world, He said: "Sacrifice and offering You did not desire, But a body You have prepared for Me.

Hebrews 10:5 NKJV

LETS GO DEEP!

Take a few moments and tell Jesus how grateful you are for His perfect sacrifice.

_____

_____

_____

_____

_____

_____

LETS GO DEEPER.

See your sin absorbed in the body of Jesus. How do you feel knowing your Heavenly Father will never remember your sins again?

_____

_____

_____

_____

_____

_____

See your shame absorbed in the body of Jesus. What does that mean to you? How can you live your life differently now?

_____

_____

_____

_____

_____

_____

_____

_____

_____

See your sickness absorbed in the body of Jesus. What does that mean to you? How can you live differently now?

_____

_____

_____

_____

_____

_____

_____

_____

_____

_____

_____

_____

_____

_____

_____

_____

_____

_____

NEW Covenant Life.

In Him you were also circumcised with the circumcision made without hands, by putting off the body of the sins of the flesh, by the circumcision of Christ, buried with Him in baptism, in which you also were raised with Him through faith in the working of God, who raised Him from the dead.

And you, being dead in your trespasses and the uncircumcision of your flesh, He has made alive together with Him, having forgiven you all trespasses, having wiped out the handwriting of requirements that was against us, which was contrary to us. And He has taken it out of the way, having nailed it to the cross. Having disarmed principalities and powers, He made a public spectacle of them, triumphing over them in it.

Colossians 2:11-15 NKJV

YOU HAVE BEEN RAISED TO NEW LIFE IN CHRIST

Your heavenly Father raised Christ from the grave by the power of the Holy Spirit.

Jesus rose without your sin, shame, and sickness. Therefore, you can be assured they do not belong to you anymore.

When Jesus rose, you rose with Him. He has been glorified and seated at the right hand of the Father far above all principality and power.

If then you were raised with Christ, seek those things which are above, where Christ is, sitting at the right hand of God. Set your mind on things above, not on things on the earth. For you died, and your life is hidden with Christ in God. When Christ who is our life appears, then you also will appear with Him in glory. Colossians 3:1-4 NKJV

PROMISES OF GOD THROUGH FAITH

As a believer in Jesus, You are now justified by faith in the work of Christ Jesus. Therefore, God has declared you righteous, and His perfect righteousness has been transferred to your account.

Through your righteous standing before God under the new covenant of grace, you can be assured that the promises of God are yours in Christ Jesus.

Furthermore, by faith in Christ, Abraham's seed, you are now heirs of the world.

For what does the Scripture say? "Abraham believed God, and it was accounted to him for righteousness." Now to him who works, the wages are not counted as grace but as debt. Romans 4:3-4 NKJV

God's promises include health, healing, blessed relationships, prosperity in all you touch, wisdom, peace with God, and more!

Let's continue reading in Romans four about how our assurance of God's promises comes through faith in Christ's finished work.

For the promise that he would be the heir of the world was not to Abraham or to his seed through the law, but through the righteousness of faith. For if those who are of the law are heirs, faith is made void and the promise made of no effect, because the law brings about wrath; for where there is no law there is no transgression.

Therefore it is of faith that it might be according to grace, so that the promise might be sure to all the seed, not only to those who are of the law, but also to those who are of the faith of Abraham, who is the father of us all. Romans 4:13-16 NKJV

Through faith you can be assured the promises of God in your life are assured. *For all the promises of God in Him are Yes, and in Him Amen, to the glory of God through us.* (1 Corinthians 1:20 NKJV)

Seated In Christ.

But God, who is rich in mercy, because of His great love with which He loved us, even when we were dead in trespasses, made us alive together with Christ (by grace you have been saved), and raised us up together, and made us sit together in the heavenly places in Christ Jesus, that in the ages to come He might show the exceeding riches of His grace in His kindness toward us in Christ Jesus.

Ephesians 2:4-7 NKJV

LETS GO DEEP!

See yourself seated in Christ in heavenly places. What does that mean to you? How can you live differently now?

_____

_____

_____

_____

_____

_____

LETS GO DEEPER.

Describe one area in your life that does not look like heaven.

_____

_____

_____

_____

_____

_____

_____

Invite Jesus into that area and ask Him what He is saying about the situation. Record it here.

_____

_____

_____

_____

_____

_____

_____

_____

_____

Begin to declare what Jesus is speaking over your life. Record the results here.

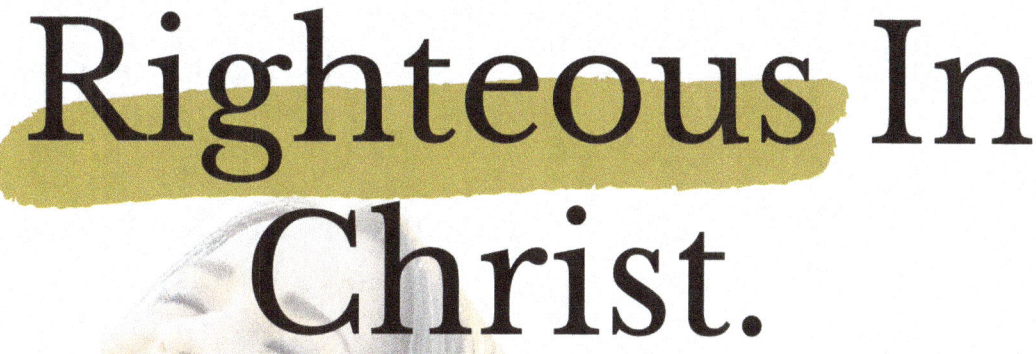

Righteous In Christ.

In righteousness you shall be established;
You shall be far from oppression, for you shall not fear;
And from terror, for it shall not come near you.

Isaiah 54:14 NKJV

CHRISTINA PERERA MINISTRIES

GOD'S RIGHTEOUSNESS BRINGS PEACE

The righteousness of God is a gift for all who believe in Christ. All that Jesus has done is set to your account, and because His righteousness is credited to you by faith, you can never lose this precious gift.

The Bible declares in the book of Romans that we will reign in life through Christ because of the abundance of grace and the gift of righteousness.

For if by the one man's offense death reigned through the one, much more those who receive abundance of grace and of the gift of righteousness will reign in life through the One, Jesus Christ. Romans 5:17 NKJV

When we reign in life as Christ, we are no longer subject to decay, sin, sickness, and death.

SPIRIT OF LIFE

Instead, the spirit of life, the Holy Spirit, reigns within us, causing life and life abundantly to spring forth.

But if the Spirit of Him who raised Jesus from the dead dwells in you, He who raised Christ from the dead will also give life to your mortal bodies through His Spirit who dwells in you. Romans 8:11 NKJV

When Jesus walked the earth, He made it abundantly clear that His heart is for you to have and experience life in every area. He stated in John, *I have come that they might have life and life abundantly.* (John10:10 NKJV)

We see Jesus healing all manner of diseases and prospering people wherever He went.

And Jesus went about all Galilee, teaching in their synagogues, preaching the gospel of the kingdom, and healing all kinds of sickness and all kinds of disease among the people. Then His fame went throughout all Syria; and they brought to Him all sick people who were afflicted with various diseases and torments, and those who were demon-possessed, epileptics, and paralytics; and He healed them. Matthew 4:23-24 NKJV

The gospels never show Jesus giving someone sickness or disease. The only people who found fault with Jesus' healing were the Pharisees.

The heart of God is unequivolcally clear that as God's beloved child He wants you well. The apostle John prays, "Beloved, I wish above all things that you prosper and be in health, even as your soul is prospering. (3 John 1:2 NKJV)

Righteousness leads to LIFE.

There is therefore now no condemnation to those who are in Christ Jesus.

Romans 8:1 NKJV

LETS GO DEEP!

Thank the Lord Jesus for the gift of His righteousness in your life! How does knowing you are righteous change the way you interact with Him?

_____

_____

_____

_____

_____

_____

LETS GO DEEPER.

What is a place you have recently fallen short? Begin to boldly declare that Christ is your righteousness here.

_____

_____

_____

_____

_____

_____

Knowing that Christ is your righteousness here how does that change the situation for you?

_____

_____

_____

_____

_____

_____

_____

_____

_____

_____

Jesus offers the gift of no condemnation. Journal about what it means for there to be no more condemnation to you in Christ.

Power of Communion.

For I received from the Lord that which I also delivered to you: that the Lord Jesus on the same night in which He was betrayed took bread; and when He had given thanks, He broke it and said, "Take, eat; this is My body which is broken for you; do this in remembrance of Me." In the same manner He also took the cup after supper, saying, "This cup is the new covenant in My blood. This do, as often as you drink it, in remembrance of Me." For as often as you eat this bread and drink this cup, you proclaim the Lord's death till He comes.

1 Corinthians 11:23-26 NKJV

REMEMBER JESUS

On the night Jesus was betrayed, He instituted what we now call the Lord's Supper or communion. He gave all believers the right to come to His table and feast on His body and blood. He instructs us to partake of this covenant meal in remembrance of Him.

For I received from the Lord that which I also delivered to you: that the Lord Jesus on the same night in which He was betrayed took bread; and when He had given thanks, He broke it and said, "Take, eat; this is My body which isbroken for you; do this in remembrance of Me."

In the same manner He also took the cup after supper, saying, "This cup is the new covenant in My blood. This do, as often as you drink it, in remembrance of Me."For as often as you eat this bread and drink this cup, you proclaim the Lord's death till He comes.
1 Corinthians 11:23-26 NKJV

DISTINGUISH BETWEEN THE BREAD & CUP

When we remember Him this way we proclaim to all the powers of darkness around us that the Lord's death has availed for us. We are simply coming into agreement with the truth of Jesus' finished work.

The proper way to remember Him is to be conscious of what these elements represent to the believer.

The bread, which represents the body of Christ broken for our healing, is essential to receiving the divine health that Jesus paid for us to have. With the bread, we are declared healed.

The prophet Isaiah prophesied that the coming new covenant instituted by the Messiah, Jesus, would accomplish our healing.

But He was pierced for our offenses, He was crushed for our wrongdoings;

The punishment for our well-being was laid upon Him, And by His wounds we are healed. Isaiah 53:5 NJKV

The cup, which represents the blood of Christ shed for your sin, is essential as with it, we are declared righteous and clean before God.

As a result of the anguish of His soul, He will see it and be satisfied; By His knowledge the Righteous One, My Servant, will justify the many, For He will bear their wrongdoings. Isaiah 53:11 NKJV

All of your sins were punished in the body of Christ; therefore, there is no more punishment for you as a believer.

All of us, like sheep, have gone astray, Each of us has turned to his own way; But the LORD has caused the wrongdoing of us all To fall on Him. Isaiah 56:6 NKJV

Discern the Body & Blood.

Take a few moments to gather some communion elements and your Bible. Read Isaiah 53, the entire messianic prophecy, and ask the Holy Spirit to open your eyes to see Jesus in it.

But this Man, after He had offered one sacrifice for sins forever, sat down at the right hand of God, from that time waiting till His enemies are made His footstool. For by one offering He has perfected forever those who are being sanctified.

Hebrews 10:12-14 NKJV

LETS GO DEEP!

Thank Jesus for His broken body (bread) for your healing. See Jesus' body broken for your healing. Write about it here.

_____

_____

_____

_____

_____

_____

_____

LETS GO DEEPER.

Thank Jesus for His blood (cup) shed for your forgiveness of sin. See, Jesus' blood cleans you now. What does being clean mean to you?

_____

_____

_____

_____

_____

Take a few moments to stay in the presence of the Lord and allow Him to minister to you. Record what is happening here.

_____

_____

_____

_____

_____

_____

_____

_____

Journal about what it means for you to remember Jesus as you take communion.

_____

_____

_____

_____

_____

_____

_____

_____

_____

_____

_____

_____

_____

_____

_____

_____

_____

_____

Freely Receive.

Heal the sick, cleanse the lepers, raise the dead, cast out demons. Freely you have received, freely give.

Matthew 10:8 NKJV

NEW COVENANT GRACE

The cross of Jesus Christ is the place of divine exchange. Through the cross, Jesus established the new covenant of the grace of Christ, one where the mercy of God met the justice of God. He could not simply sweep our sin and sickness under the rug. Instead, He became our offering of sacrifice to pay the penalty for every believer once and for all.

Previously saying, "Sacrifice and offering, burnt offerings, and offerings for sin You did not desire, nor had pleasure in them" (which are offered according to the law), then He said, "Behold, I have come to do Your will, O God." He takes away the first that He may establish the second. By that will we have been sanctified through the offering of the body of Jesus Christ once for all. Hebrews 10:8-10 NJKV

On the cross, Jesus unleashed the free-flowing grace of God for all who will believe.

JESUS PAID THE PRICE FOR YOUR TOTAL HEALING

He received the scouraging necessary to bring healing to your body. He wore the crown of thorns for your mind to be at peace. He cried out in separation from the Father so you and I can draw close to God without fear.

*Surely He has borne our griefs
And carried our sorrows;
Yet we esteemed Him stricken,
Smitten by God, and afflicted.
But He was wounded for our transgressions, He was bruised for our iniquities;
The chastisement for our peace was upon Him,
And by His stripes we are healed. All we like sheep have gone astray; We have turned, every one, to his own way;
And the Lord has laid on Him the iniquity of us all.*
Isaiah 53:4-6 NKJV

The sinless Son of God received your sin so that you can receive His righteousness.

Now then, we are ambassadors for Christ, as though God were pleading through us: we implore you on Christ's behalf, be reconciled to God. For He made Him who knew no sin to be sin for us, that we might become the righteousness of God in Him.
2 Corinthians 5:20-21 NKJV

All that remains is for you to receive your healing by faith freely. Know that though the finished work of Jesus your redemption is complete. There is nothing you need to do to add to His work. All that remains is for you to believe and receive.

So Jesus answered and said to them, "Have faith in God. For assuredly, I say to you, whoever says to this mountain, 'Be removed and be cast into the sea,' and does not doubt in his heart, but believes that those things he says will be done, he will have whatever he says. Therefore I say to you, whatever things you ask when you pray, believe that you receive them, and you will have them.
Mark 11:22-24 NKJV

By Grace, through Faith.

Take a few moments to come before the Lord Jesus by faith. Begin to acknowledge your need before Him and thank Him for the healing already accomplished for you.

Let us therefore come boldly to the throne of grace, that we may obtain mercy and find grace to help in time of need.

Hebrews 4:16 NKJV

LETS GO DEEP!

Thank Jesus for recieving your sickness through the scouraging on the whipping post. Write about it here.

_____

_____

_____

_____

_____

_____

LETS GO DEEPER.

Thank Jesus for recieving your sin on the cross. See, Jesus' wearing the crown of thorns for you. Write about it here.

_____

_____

_____

_____

_____

_____

Take a few moments to stay in the presence of the Lord and allow Him to minister to you. Record what is happening here.

_____

_____

_____

_____

_____

_____

_____

_____

_____

Journal about what it means stand on the Word of God and finished work of Jesus to receive your healing by faith.

_____

_____

_____

_____

_____

_____

_____

_____

_____

_____

_____

_____

_____

_____

_____

_____

_____

_____

Resources.

Bless the Lord, O my soul;
And all that is within me, bless His holy name!
Bless the Lord, O my soul,
And forget not all His benefits:
Who forgives all your iniquities,
Who heals all your diseases,
Who redeems your life from destruction,
Who crowns you with lovingkindness and tender mercies,
Who satisfies your mouth with good things,
So that your youth is renewed like the eagle's.

Psalm 103:1-5 NKJV

PRAYER OF HEALING

Father,

I thank you for the incredible gift of your Son, Jesus. As a believer, I am a child of God, fully forgiven, righteous, and loved by you. Jesus is my savior, healer, and deliverer; by His stripes, I was healed.

I now call forth my healing in Christ. May the full manifestation of the high price paid for me be seen in my entire being today.

I declare by faith that my mind, body, and soul are healed in Jesus. I command everything that tries to come against this knowledge of Jesus' finished work to leave now.

I speak to my body, and I command that you come into alignment with the finished work of Christ and the Word of God. I release the shalom peace of God throughout my body, mind, and soul now.

In the mighty name of Jesus,
Amen

SCAN FOR VIDEO PRAYER

PRACTICAL TIPS TO HEALING

Healing can be an immediate event or a process, but Jesus has guaranteed your healing based on His Word. Continue renewing your mind. Be sure to follow the leading of your medical professional as you build your faith for healing.

☐ **LISTEN TO HEALING TESTIMONIES**
There is power in hearing testimonies of God's healing power today. Every time a testimony is shared, it opens the door for God to do it again in your life.

☐ **READ PASSAGES ON HEALING**
The gospels—Matthew, Mark, Luke, and John — contain accounts of Jesus healing many. The Book of Acts contains testimonies of the apostles healing in Jesus' name.

☐ **LISTEN TO MESSAGES CENTERED ON JESUS**
Listen to messages all about the person and work of Jesus, such as *Revealing Jesus with Christina Perera*.

☐ **MAKE IT A HABIT TO SPEND TIME WITH JESUS EVERYDAY**
You can speak to God the way you would a person. He is always with you and willing to listen. Read your Bible and journal what He is speaking/teaching you.

☐ **WORSHIP & PRAYER ARE POWERFUL**
Anytime you worship God, His presence manifests around you, driving out all darkness and disease and fighting your every enemy. Singing, praying, and giving thanks are all forms of worship.

☐ **TAKE COMMUNION DAILY**
You are a priest in God's eyes, and one of the most potent New Testament ways of receiving healing is through Holy Communion. Please take it as often as you need.

☐ **SHARE YOUR TESTIMONY**
There is power in sharing your testimony with others. You open the door for God to move in another persons life.

MEDICAL DISCLAIMER

The information in this book is for educational purposes only and is not intended to substitute for professional medical advice. If you or a loved one have a medical concern, you should consult medical professionals for medical advice, diagnosis, or treatment. As always, we encourage you to seek the Lord for His wisdom and guidance in every situation. You should not stop taking any medications without speaking to a medical professional first. While we make no guarantees, please understand that individuals may experience different levels of results. We continue to stand in faith, affirming God's Word, and believe in healing with you.

Hey! I'm "Christina"

My heart desires to see the people of God receive all Jesus died to give them. As a five-fold minister, revivalist, author, and speaker with a fiery passion for Jesus that spreads like wildfire, I carry the revelation of the gospel of Jesus Christ. I long to bring the body of Christ into the fullness of the finished work of Jesus and see each one of us reach a hurting world with love. It is a great honor to encourage others in the goodness of God.

I sincerely hope this resource has blessed your relationship with God and deepened your walk with Him. I would love to keep in touch and continue encouraging you in the things of God!

We would love to hear how this resource has blessed you. Please leave a review on Amazon to help others know how it has blessed you. You can follow us on social media at @christinapereraministres on Facebook & Instagram. Listen to hear more about our beautiful Savior Jesus on *Revealing Jesus With Christina Perera* wherever you get your podcasts.

LET'S KEEP IN TOUCH
Visit Us Online Here

MORE RESOURCES

REVEALING JESUS WITH CHRISTINA PERERA:
Available on all podcast platforms and
YouTube@christinapereraministries

NEW BELIEVER WORKBOOK & JOURNAL:
Foundational Gospel Truths to Begin Your
Relationship With Christ Jesus.
Available at ChristinaPerera.org/store and Amazon

**AT THE FEET OF JESUS
WORSHIP & PRAYER JOURNAL:**
Available at ChristinaPerera.org/store and Amazon

JESUS CENTERED FAITH-FILLED TEACHING:
Available at ChristinaPerera.org/blog

www.ingramcontent.com/pod-product-compliance
Lightning Source LLC
Chambersburg PA
CBHW081347120626
46546CB00011B/3477